The Abyss

Robert Otken

Presentation by *BookLeaf Publishing*

Web: www.bookleafpub.com

E-mail: info@bookleafpub.com

ISBN: 9789357616027

First edition 2022

ACKNOWLEDGEMENT

Thanks I have to give to Bethany Reys for proofreading all my poetic exclamations, telling me off when I got too political or too self-indulgent. As an author it is always difficult to put your creations out to the public, and a non-judgemental proof reader is the best way to start doing so.

Of course all poems here are just writings from my mind. Even with all our editing and proofreading there might still have slipped in some minor errors. I hope they are not too distracting. And if you do get lost, remember, we are not lost, we are on an adventure!

PREFACE

"To be nobody but yourself in a world which is doing its best day and night to make you like everybody else means to fight the hardest battle which any human being can fight and never stop fighting" E.E. Cummings

This short collection of 21 poems just came into being after some foraging in the deep dark abyss of my mind. It was a bit of a challenge to write these as I haven't really forayed into poetry much before.

What I tried to achieve with each of these is portray a feeling, or some small kernel of wisdom. Poetry is art, and art is a vessel of expression. It might not have iambic pentameter or sonnet form or anything else poetry can have, but each one has been written with intent. Many poems here will echo the sentiment expressed in the E.E. Cummings quote at the top of the page. To live a life of freedom and happiness, in peace, is the ultimate goal of humanity. Hopefully leaving the world a better place than we found it.

Poetry is not designed to be read once or fast, therefore I encourage you to read it slowly, and ponder the words and meaning. Maybe you can find a bit more than just the mere words.

One day at a time

One day at a time
Step by step I climb
Out of the deep dark pit
All the nasty grey grit
My hands are being scratched
Dark red blood patched
It is so easy to give up
Slide back down in the grub
Be covered in the nasty mess
Don't think of you any less
Just to be fair
It is not easy to climb
Out of the pit of despair
After wallowing in my pain
I have to try again
Be cream of the crop
I can reach the top

Stuck

Why do I feel stuck?
Am I out of luck?
They say I can do all things
With love under my wings
Trapped in this cage I cannot fly
Oh, Universe please answer me why.
Is it me who is chaining me down
Acting like the Devil's clown
Where is the progress?
I just seem to make a mess
People do not understand
No, I do not need a hand
I need to rest my soul
Before I turn into a ghoul
Once I lay my body to rest
On a beach, so I can test
The waves rolling over me
Ow, what joy, to be free
Let go of the self inflicted cage
You do not have to be a mage
I can choose to open the door
Let the light shine in, as before
Chase away the dark shadows
Depression she verily knows
She has no choice but to flee
As soon as I set myself free!

DIY

With a stumble and a little stagger
It takes a little skill
I fall back on my own dagger

I am just me, and not him, Mick Jagger
Let's take that bitter pill
I fall back on my own dagger

Normally I am not a big bragger
If looks could surely kill
I fall back on my own dagger

Although I am very much a lagger
Clearly I've had my fill
I fall back on my own dagger

Banned books

They are banning the books
Not for their good looks
Does reading Josef Conrad
Really make you mad?
Books, as a rule of thumb
Do not keep you dumb
They banned 1984
Heaven knows what for
A book did not make me gay
Luckily, I was born this way
Maybe I am sentimental
But reading is fundamental
Books quite contrary
Run to the library
They teach you history, fast
Reading about mistakes past
Books are a better teacher
Than many a religious preacher
But once you get smart
Controlling you, will be hard
So if that is what you want
Banning books is grand
Read about Peter Pan
He will never become a man
In a similar manner

also the book banner
Humanity will forget
That's the great regret
Read all banned literature
Don't become a caricature
To be or not to be
Shakespeare has asked
It is up to you, and me
Humanity has been tasked
Broaden your own mind
And see if you can find
To be part of human kind

True

Be true to yourself
That is the best
Books on the shelf
Help with the rest
Follow your hearts desire
Forge your own path
Get your brain to rewire
Give your soul a bath
Wash off the training
The societal indoctrination
Behavioural ingraining
Spiritual divination
After all the brainwashing
Instagram and Facebook
Information smashing
Everything is gobbledegook

Bitten

What is wrong with people
If you give them a finger
They take your whole hand
Break your heart
And optimism
Making you never want
To give anything again

If you are not giving
You are an egoist
Everytime you go the extra mile
You get taken for a ride
society is making you
A nasty selfish person
Twice bitten once shy

Humans are giving mixed signals
No wonder no one understands
Humankind lost its kind
Stop caring about others
Their opinion does not matter
Be your own biggest fan
Rule in the kingdom of your mind
Build the walls, dig the moats
Do not let the evil them in

Protect your soul from harm
You, just you, are enough

Grey

The sky is a murky dark grey
Rain plummeting down in my heart
When will this coldness leave
Younglings want to grow up
To be an adult. To live life
Now all the grey skies
Make me want to die

So much effort wasted
We are insignificant specks
dust in the multiverse
Convergence of universal consciousness
Spiritually connected to all
Like one long bad acid trip
Colours dancing together
Forming a grey murky mess

Words

Words transform a life
Creativity flows
Stories bubble to the top
People die, fall in love
Solve or commit crimes,
or do random stuff
Letters, dashes and hooks
Symbols and sounds merging
To words, sentences, stories
Every tone, harmony, frequency
Working together to create
Poetry, novel, a symphony

Letting go of your writing
Is like having a child
You want it to do good
In the world
But it just as well
Might flop, become hell
All I can do is
Make it as good
As possible, teach it well
And it will find a way
Life is like an IKEA cupboard
Others make it look very easy

But when doing it yourself
It never turns out as it should

Smithing with words
Like an alchemist with elements
A drop of silvery mercury
Pool of heavy water
Primordial tomato soup
Atoms and electrons
From dust to dust
All building blocks.
A castle made from Lego
With one pink block amidst the grey
A puzzle with one piece missing
Art is a vessel of self expression
To recreate the missing piece
Sacrificing a small piece of yourself

Emotion

Anger pops up like grey mist
Deep in the majestic forest
Dew on the morning nettles
There is no stopping it
A force of nature to be reckoned with

The emotion infiltrates every pore
It takes over control of the whole being
An alien bursts out of the abdomen
Out of control the human screams
A horror movie, a cheap drama plot

Life is a collection of emotions
Each plays it's own unique role
There is no good or bad, it just is
The world is your petri dish
Your oyster, your runway.

Resistance is Futile

We are born, male or female
Placed into a box immediately
Resistance is futile
You will be assimilated

Do not be different,
Peer pressure will direct you
Resistance is futile
You will be assimilated

Conform to the standards
The social guidelines
Resistance is futile
You will be assimilated

Jesus died for our sins
Except if you are...
Resistance is futile
You will be assimilated

At birth placed in a box
At death into another box
Resistance is futile
You will be assimilated

Watch Hollywood movies
American tv dramas
Resistance is futile
You will be assimilated

Globalisation, small town world
Cultures all becoming similar
Resistance is futile
You will be assimilated

Like a drop of blue ink
In a bucket of clear water
Resistance is futile
You will be assimilated

Don't stand out,
No tall poppies
Resistance is futile
You will be assimilated

Stop the assimilation
Conformity is boring
It is the divergence
That makes the world a better place
Cheese fondue of cultures
To dip your white bread in
Humans off the world rise up
Embrace colourful diversity
Don't assimilate into the grey

Resistance is worth it
You will become free!

The wall

I built my own wall
Brick by brick
Layer by layer
In stretcher bond
Or stylish Flemish
A soldier course on top
To protect myself
No one can get in
Nothing can hurt me
Safe within these walls
Maybe some glass shards
Or barbed wire above it
Keep the evil out
Only trouble is
If no one can get in
I will be alone, forever lonely
Behind my stretcher bond wall
With glass shards and barbed wire
Feelings will fester
Unable to release,
Blocked in by the wall
Slowly suffocating myself

Destroy

This big ball spinning
Round a fiery bigger ball
Speck of dust in the universe
But it is our grain of sand
Human influence is burning up
Our fossil fuels, tropical rain forests
Greenhouse effect warming up
Like a cold scoop of ice
Left out in the sun too long
Once the earth melts it is over.
From dust to a speck of dust in the universe
As the earth warms up
Becomes uninhabitable
Which planet shall we destroy next?

Work

Another hard earned dollar
Another day wasted away
All my money is spent
At least i paid my rent

Another long day to toil
Away on this mortal coil
Working eight to five
Extra hours, excluding drive

Another day slaving away
Earning barely minimum wage
No more money to spent
Drink a cheaper blend

Another day another dollar
Where is the fun?
Life is wasting away
Go out and play!

Another life you don't get
Spend this one wisely
Life is too short
To waste being bored

Do not live to only work
load to much on y'r fork
you can work tomorrow, don't fret
Live life now without regret.

Another day another sorrow
You'd better work tomorrow
Today set aside to play
If there is a will, you will find a way.

Another day another hour
Step inside your power
Just let go, And let God
Work His magic in your life

Another day another stanza
Another line of poetry mangled
Shut up and just stop writing
Switch, maybe i should take up knitting?

Bold

Go on, step up and walk into the light
Do not hesitate, do not be afraid
The clear summer morning early and bright
Open your heart, do not be dismayed

Step up, set a new standard
You do measure up, reach the top
Life will bring problems: easy and hard
You can make it, plant a new crop

Be bold be strong and step out of the shadows
All you need is within you right now
The world is your runway, no reason to hide

Be bold be strong and step into the light
 Spread your wings and take flight

Word flow

Words tumbling out
Of my mouth
Like a waterfall
The previously blank page
Filling up with ramblings
Blisters on my feet
From running a marathon
Blisters on my soul
From drinking a marathon
The creative juices flow
Filling up the blank page
Was it worth the hangover
Get the words out
Write them down immediately
So I do not forget
Tomorrow I can edit it all
Like a traditional artist
On Absinthe or alcohol
I will not cut off my ear
The words ejaculate
On to the not so blank page
Breaking the dam made of
inadequacy, fear of failure
You cannot edit an empty page
So let the words flow

A marathon of emotions
A string of events
Every step taken
Every word written
Brings you closer to the finish

Spring

The sun is out
Yellow rays of warming light
Heating the ground
My black rough floor surface
Warming my feet, my heart

The sun is out
The Michelin men
Disappear from the streets
The milk bottles underneath
The denim shorts appear

The sun is out
come out of the closet
Spring has sprung
Leave the cold of winter behind
Step out into the yellow sunlight

The sun is out
Flowers peek through the soil
The world becomes
More colourful, more alive
Re-birthing of happiness

Jacuzzi

Sitting in my jacuzzi
Portable lazy spa
Outdoor, on the balcony
Soaking up the warming rays
From the yellow fiery ball above
A white five pointed star
Floating on the water
Filtering the rubbish
From the water mirror

Bubbles floating up
Towards the hot glowing sun
Caressing my nakedness
Full frontal freedom
No clothing to wear me down
Does life get any better?

Underneath the burning Australian sun
There is one more way to improve
Upon lazy spa perfection
Being naked together
With you, my love, so
Let us rejoice, and soak in it!

Pearls

Little pleasures in life
It is in the moments of decision
That your destiny is created
Tea, earl grey, hot
Flavoured with Bergamot
A relaxing sip to unwind
It is moments like these
That make me thrive
Your own decisions create life
No one else to blame, but yourself...
Life is a String of pearls
Moments of joy, of pleasure
Moments of intense happiness
Moments of pain and deep hurt
All strung together on
the lifelong cord of breath.
Savour the moments
Those are the ones you will remember.
Slow down and be present
In the current moment
Think how you can make this moment better
Decide, and do it now.

Revolution

Start with some corpse pose
Lying dead still on the floor
Emptying your cup
Only ground stains are left
Soul connecting to the universe
Through the looking glass
Consciousness to consciousness
Energy flows where focus goes
Focus on your physical presence
Cat cow pose, maybe some pigeon?
Shiver me timbers and call me hooked
Find your inner warrior
Samurai fighter on your behalf
Strong, fierce able to deal with life
Learn on the mat, live it off the mat.
Inhale lots of love and exhale lots of love,
Breath life into your being.
No more sleeping with the past,
Or flirting with the future
Flawless Unsurpassable Classy Knockout
Worthy Irresistible Talented
Feel all giddy inside, happy baby
I might pass out with excitement
Just be...
A mountain, present in the present.

Self doubt

Shut up self doubt
We are going to kick arse
All my personalities
Align and work together
To prove you wrong
With some self talk
You're never alone
Learn the proper words
To describe yourself
Awesome is one of those
Fantastic, fierce and funny
Love is patient, love is kind
The wind rises
Tearing dead leaves free
Removing self doubt
We often fear what we do not understand
Our best defence is knowledge
Know the truth
And the truth will set you free.

Dare to live

Now I am the voice
Speaking with an ancient wisdom
Directing my destiny

I will lead not follow
Through the jungle
Forge my own path

I will create not destroy
Build my castle in the sky
If I can dream it, I can achieve it

A force for good
Dare to dream; allow to be
Leaving a better world in our wake

Step up to the plate
Hit it out of the park
Your life: a homerun

Set a new standard
Don't accept anything less
You create the rules

Manifest your destiny

Your dreams and thoughts
Create your life.